A JOURNEY INTO THE ICY HEART OF THE WHITE CONTINENT

BHUPENDER GUPTA

ISBN 979-8-89133-921-7

DEDICATION

To my dearest friends and well-wishers,

You have been the compass guiding me through the vast, uncharted landscapes of my literary pursuits. With each step of this journey, your unwavering support has warmed the coldest of Antarctic winds, and your belief in me has melted the most formidable icebergs of doubt.

This book, like the boundless expanse of Antarctica, is a testament to the power of community, friendship, and the belief that dreams can be achieved. With your confidence and encouragement, I have found the courage to venture into the realms of words and stories, and it is with immense gratitude that I dedicate this work to you all.

May this book be a small token of my appreciation for your kindness and faith in me. As we explore the mysteries of Antarctica together within these pages, may it also serve as a reminder that with friends like you by my side, there are no limits to what we can achieve.

With heartfelt thanks,

Bhupender Gupta.

Contents

Acknowledgments

I extend my sincere gratitude to Notion Press, a beacon of professionalism and commitment in the world of publishing. You have not only transformed my words into beautifully crafted books but have also played a vital role in bringing them into the spotlight of the literary stage.

Your dedication to quality, attention to detail, and unwavering support have been instrumental in shaping my journey as an author. From the very first manuscript to this fourth book on Antarctica, you have consistently exceeded my expectations, ensuring that each word found its rightful place on the pages, and each book became a work of art.

It is a privilege to work with a publisher that shares my passion for literature and storytelling. Your team's hard work, from editing to cover design, from distribution to promotion, has been nothing short of exceptional. Together, we have ventured into the world of words, and I am grateful for the partnership that has made this journey possible.

To Notion Press, thank you for being more than a publisher; you have been a partner, a collaborator, and a friend on this literary expedition. I look forward to many more adventures together as we continue to share stories with the world.

With deep appreciation

Bhupender Gupta

Synopsis

This book is about my recent trip to Antarctica and my travel experiences there. It describes the day-to-day travel experience during the 14-day voyage to the Antarctica peninsula, beginning in Santiago, Chile's capital, and continuing by air to Port Williams, the last city on Earth, and then boarding the Silver Seas cruise for a captivating 14-day tour of the world's white continent. The author's exciting encounters with Antarctica's fauna, breathtaking vistas, and captivating icebergs are neatly chronicled para by para, coupled with photographs taken by the author himself, to make the text more informative and understandable.

It is a travelogue that will allow readers to experience these destinations vicariously through the author.

Introduction

In a world where adventure knows no bounds, there exists a realm of pristine beauty and unforgiving wilderness—a place so remote and untamed that it remains an enigma to most and where glaciers loom like ancient sentinels, and the air is imbued with a palpable sense of primordial mystery. This is the story of my sojourn to the ethereal White Continent- Antarctica, a chronicle of moments etched in ice, where the very notion of time seems suspended, and reality itself takes on the guise of a dream.

Join me as I weave a tale of awe-inspiring landscapes, breathtaking encounters with wildlife, and the sheer exhilaration of venturing into the heart of an icy realm where the ordinary rules of travel cease to apply. In this narrative, you will witness the extraordinary, and perhaps even catch a glimpse of the profound changes that come when one steps foot on the frozen shores of a land untouched by time. Welcome to my odyssey to Antarctica, where every step feels like a brushstroke on the canvas of a forgotten world, an invitation to embrace the extraordinary.

Trip to the White Continent

As you settle into your seat on a *British Airways* flight from *Mumbai* to *Santiago*, your heart beats a symphony of excitement and anxiety. A tapestry of clouds and azure horizons beckons you to an ambitious adventure as you gaze out your window to the world beyond. The purpose is to embark on an adventurous adventure that will take you to the extreme limit of human exploration—the enigmatic land of *Antarctica*.

You've arrived in *Santiago, Chile's* capital city, on the suggestion of an amiable gentleman named *Mr John Ambat*, a representative of your shipping firm, *Silver Seas*, in India. Excitement for your journey to the White Continent *(one of Earth's seven continents. Now probably Eighth after the International scientists have discovered 'Zealandia')* is running through your veins, as is a willingness to leap headfirst into an adventure that promises nothing short of fantastic.

Saludos desde Santiago *(Greetings from Santiago)*

The luxurious *Hotel Mandarin Oriental* is an instant destination upon arrival in *Santiago*, a haven amid the busy downtown. Once inside the hotel's spacious lobby, you present yourself to the Silver Seas Cruises staff filled with confidence and excitement.

Following the completion of the papers, you enter a reasonably spacious room where you can relax and prepare for the adventure ahead.

Embracing Culinary Delights

Later, to prepare your senses for exploring the unexplored territory, you now decide to fuel up at the nearby vegan eatery called *'Indian Box'*.

Spices flood the air as you sit in to savor a non-fish *Goan curry* expertly paired with aromatic jeera rice giving the traditional Indian fare a modern makeover. The resulting tastes are an inexplicable party on your tongue. Their unique juice is a refreshing blend that perfectly complements the meal and leaves you feeling full.

The White Continent's Call

As you enjoy your meal in this vegan utopia, your thoughts wander to the majesty of *Antarctica*. The very thought of its clean, unspoiled, and breathtaking scenery is enough to stir your soul. You're glad that you shall see the seventh continent of the world when so few people ever get the chance to.

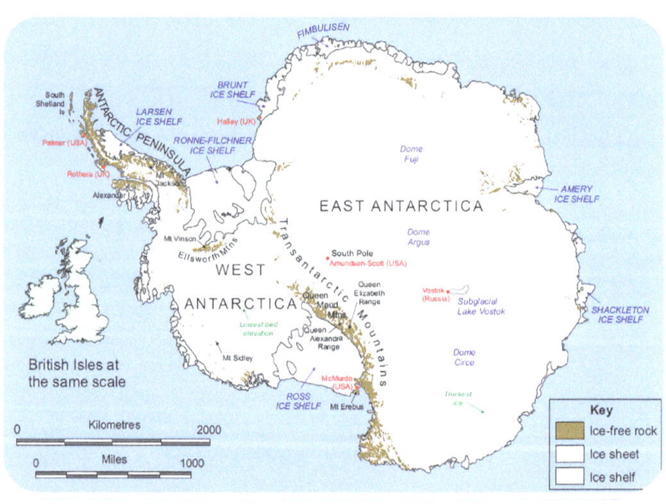

Image credit: British Antarctic Survey

At Earth's southernmost tip, *Antarctica,* as you learn, is a vast ice continent with a unique terrain and a thick ice sheet covering approximately 98% of its land area. This 2,000-meter-thick *(6,600-foot-thick)* ice sheet, surrounded by the *Southern Ocean,* reportedly stores over 70% of the world's fresh water. Several mountain ranges dotting the icy continent's surface, include the *Trans-Antarctic Mountains* that run roughly east to west across the continent.

The *South Pole* is roughly at 90 degrees south latitude; however, Antarctica spans a far larger range of latitudes. The *Antarctic Circle,* defined as the area south of 66.5 degrees latitude, envelops this continent. Because of Antarctica's position on the prime meridian, the entire continent may be crossed from east to west at any latitude between 0 and 180 degrees.

After refuelling your body and soul, you now head back to the *Mandarin Oriental* for the next leg of your journey.

Tomorrow is the time to say goodbye to *Santiago* and embark on the amazing journey to *Antarctica* that awaits you after a night of unique cocktails and fine Japanese food hosted by the prominent cruise line.

As you retire for the night in your hotel room, the excitement levels are at an all-time high. Despite the journey from Mumbai to Santiago loaded with conflicting emotions, you are now on the verge of an unforgettable experience. The white continent is begging you to come and explore its untamed wilderness.

The next day, you shall set sail on the *Silver Seas Cruise,* a vessel that will take you over perilous waters and into *Antarctica's* surreal scenery. A sense of ambivalence sets up as you draw nearer to the incredible unknown. Anxiety and exhilaration start to play off one another.

Antarctic Journey: From Santiago to the Frozen Frontier

The following morning, after breakfast at the hotel, the cruise line will quickly process your checked luggage. You and your party, meanwhile, take a bus to the terminal, where you'll board a chartered flight to *Puerto Williams*, the world's most southern city and entry point to the *Antarctic Peninsula*

On Board the Private Plane

Anticipation builds as the exquisite *Antarctic Airways* jet, with room for eighty passengers, takes off from *Santiago Airport* at three o'clock in the afternoon for the four-hour flight to *Puerto Williams*.

The pilot's statement echoes through the cabin, filling you and the other fellow passengers with a sensation of excitement and awe as you fly above the gorgeous landscape.

On the way to Puerto Williams

Discovering and Exploring Puerto Williams

The seclusion and natural beauty of *Puerto Williams* hit you like a ton of bricks as you arrive at *Navarino Island* in the *Beagle Channel*.

Puerto Williams – Bay

This small town of roughly 2,500 inhabitants sits near Chile's southernmost tip and serves as a departure point for trips to Antarctica. You feel an unexplainable burst of energy as you take a deep breath of the clean air and realize that you are entering a region that has seen very few people.

Preparing for the Big Trip

While the cruise line's friendly service makes it easy for guests to transfer quickly from the waiting plane to the ship, the journey from Santiago to this remote place was arguably full of excitement, delicious food, and impeccable travel arrangements.

Getting Ready to Leave for the Frozen Frontier

Ready to leave *Puerto Williams* and head out into the icy wilderness of Antarctica, your heart is racing with excitement. The *Silver Cloud Ship*, which will carry you across the dangerous waters on this incredible journey, stands proud and elegant at the pier.

Silver Cloud Cruise Ship

Even as the ship waits for you to embark, your enthusiasm for the rare combination of magnificent scenery, fascinating wildlife, and overpowering tranquillity builds with each passing second.

Beginning of Day One on the Silver Cloud

The glittering silver ship, a gorgeous creation owned by the illustrious *Silver Seas Cruises*, promises a journey of wealth and grandeur. With space for 254 illustrious guests and a dedicated crew of 212, this floating paradise is indeed an oasis of comfort and indulgence.

Prepare to be awestruck as you step foot on this nine-deck masterpiece, where every crevice is an homage to class and refinement. The ship's suites come in a variety of sizes and styles to accommodate any traveller. There is a haven for everyone, ranging from opulent and roomy lodgings to private and quiet retreats.

You hop on the ship with delight, knowing that it will be your home for the next 13 days. Once inside, you'll find yourself among a lively group of other visitors, all of whom are about to embark on this incredible adventure with you.

Having gone through the standard check-in procedures, they hand you over the key to your veranda suite on the ship's seventh level.

As you walk into this elegant room, anticipation leads the way. Your attention is instantly pulled to the sparkling wine bottle that sits proudly in the center of the table. Its mere existence exudes class and portends celebratory evenings full of toasts.

Veranda Suite No 717

Before you know it, you're staring down at the neatly folded fleece jacket, the bright red *parka*, and the lightweight *backpack* with the coveted Silversea logo proudly displayed over them, lying on a comfortable-looking queen bed. The suite literally invites you to embrace yourself in its warmth and comfort, offering restful nights and pleasant dreams.

In one of the suite's nooks are a pair of pre-ordered custom-fit *gumboots*, waiting for you to put them on while you explore the world. Next to them is a pair of sturdy *walking sticks (poles)* that will serve as a trusty companion on expeditions across uncharted territory.

Your bags have arrived on schedule and can be seen stacked carefully in a corner, waiting for your inspection. Having them around provides you peace of mind, knowing your belongings are safe and secure.

As you sink into the sofa and allow its soft cushions to cradle your tired body, a sense of well-being washes over you. A deep sense of calm and eagerness for the glorious voyage that awaits just beyond the horizon replaces the stresses of the outside world.

Guests can enjoy delicious meals at any of the ship's four restaurants, each of which is a culinary masterpiece in its own right. At *The Grill*, you may feast on succulent steaks in an elegant atmosphere while being enchanted by *La Dame's* exquisite French cuisine. The eating experiences at both establishments are superb. At *La Terrazza*, you may sample some of the delicious cuisine of the Mediterranean with its tempting menu of dishes that highlight the region's distinctive characteristics. And your taste buds are in for a treat at *The Restaurant*, where masterful dishes are prepared to create a symphony of tastes.

There are no bounds to luxury on this ship. Relax and rejuvenate your senses with the help of the expert stylists at *Zagara Beauty Salon*. Unwind by taking a plunge in the pool on the pool deck, a tranquil oasis amid the ocean's splendour. Take advantage of the state-of-the-art fitness center so that you may maintain your regular exercise routine while away from home. In addition, if you're in the mood for some shopping therapy, the ship's boutique, *Alpaca*, has a nice selection of presents.

Restaurants and Pool on Silver Cloud Cruise Ship

The ship's sizable exploration team, under the direction of the intrepid *Mr. Scott*, has access to 20 zodiacs and 10 kayaks. They will stand ready to guide you through the awe-inspiring landscapes of *Antarctica*, unlocking its secrets and marvels and also prepare you to get captivated by the pristine beauty of this icy wonderland, as you navigate through glistening waters and encounter breathtaking wildlife.

The *Silver Cloud Ship's* lovely lounges are an essential part of any cruise experience without which your voyage cannot possibly be complete. Relax in style and comfort in the *Explorer Lounge*, while taking in amazing views from the *Observation Lounge*. Drink in the breathtaking panoramas from the *Panorama Lounge* while making memories that will last a lifetime.

You have now embarked on a journey unlike any other aboard this Ship, where luxury, adventure, and magic come together to create an adventure unlike any other.

Having placed your tripod and camera inside your suit's veranda, you have prepared yourself to capture the spectacular landscapes of Antarctica as well as all the other magical adventures that await.

Mr. Rommel and Mr. Gede, two dedicated members of the ship's crew, arrive soon to present themselves in your cabin. *Mr. Rommel,* the butler, assures to take care of your dining needs and specific demands. Meanwhile, *Mr. Gede* greets you with a pleasant smile and pledges to service your cabin at least twice daily to keep it smelling and looking great.

The ship has set sail in the dead of night, marking the beginning of an expedition to the beautiful Antarctic continent at the Earth's southernmost tip.

As the ship ploughs through the icy waters, you are overcome with appreciation for the opportunity to view the pristine splendour of the beautiful white continent.

Second Day: Going Through the Drake Passage

As the first rays of dawn light filter into your cabin, you open your eyes to a breathtaking sight. The cruise liner is currently making its way through the fabled *Drake Passage,* located between South America's *Cape Horn* and the *South Shetland Islands* of the Antarctica ocean. Area known for its dangerously rough and seemingly endless blue waters.

Since the vessel has neared the narrowest point of the channel, there is a noticeable shift. Water's usually tranquil state has transformed into a powerful force, with waves towering over 4 meters in height crashing together in turbulent patterns.

The ship is currently pitching and rolling, giving passengers a roller coaster-like sensation with a thrilling drop and a rapid ascent. It thus packed the setting with a unique blend of emotions, and each person's experience is a variety of experiences that reflect the untamed dance of the ocean below.

The primary reason for the choppy waters is because of the convergence of the Antarctic Circumpolar Current (ACC) with the warmer waters of the Atlantic and Pacific Ocean.

Unlike some other oceanic passages, there are no significant landmasses in the Drake Passage to break up the flow of ocean currents. This lack of obstruction probably allows the currents to build up speed and power, creating these chaotic gigantic waves.

As the ship travels further, so do the feelings. The relentless strength of the waves seems to test the mettle of even the most seasoned travellers, leaving them shaky. There is now a cacophony of emotions on the decks, with some people clinging to the railings with white-knuckled grips and expressions of both awe and fear, their faces pale and their eyes wide.

For many travellers, however, the thrill of crossing the *Drake Passage* and experiencing its challenging conditions is part of the adventure of visiting Antarctica.

The vastness of the ocean before you is nevertheless, an unqualified reminder of the epic trip that lies ahead. While the ship is smashing through these enormous waves, they blend the thrill of exploration with apprehension.

You, meanwhile, get plenty of opportunity to reflect on the ocean's grandeur and its untamed might. The pristine beauty of *Antarctica*, the seventh continent of the Earth, awaits you.

View from the ship

The Restaurant is open for you to indulge in a nourishing breakfast, after which you resolve to remain in your stateroom until the ship has safely passed through this testing passage. Today, thus, will be a day of complete peace and quiet.

But when the ship shines golden in the evening light, you cannot miss the rumblings of excitement. In a grand hall on Deck 5, a curious group of people have gathered in anticipation of knowing about the upcoming expeditions. Each guest is further motivated upon discovering that the accomplished and adventurous *Mr. Scott* will lead the expedition.

A brilliant assistant, *Mr. Belly*, a seasoned explorer whose passion for knowledge seems infectious, has joined *Mr. Scott*. Twelve more equally amazing individuals round out this band of intrepid souls.

It is natural to get electric energy and a sense of endless possibilities when they are around. This remarkable crew not only has the expertise to guide you through the ship's planned investigations but also the ability to ensure your safety and comfort during exciting *Zodiac boat* trips and spectacular journeys to a variety of landing sites.

These outstanding folks enthrall you as they pull you into the story. Their leadership and dedication will undoubtedly transform your getaway into an exhilarating exploration of the unknown.

Day 3: On Silver Clouds

The sun rises over the vast ocean as morning unfolds. Waves that were raging earlier have subsided, and the ship has emerged from the *Drake Passage*, providing comfort and much-needed relief from seasickness. A strong sense of accomplishment accompanies the feeling of relief as you gaze in awe at the surrounding water's grandeur.

On the way to the Antarctic Peninsula

Today, as you gather in the *Explorer Lounge* on the 5th deck for an educational lecture on Antarctica, serendipity strikes. The speaker's remarks are interrupted by an unanticipated but welcome announcement.

Whales have been sighted swimming alongside the ship. Unsurprisingly, there is a flurry of excitement as everyone prepares to dash back to their suits, hoping to glimpse these magnificent monsters.

Standing on the balcony of the suite, with alacrity, you take pictures of a breathtaking scene using your trusty camera. Majestic whales burst on the water's surface with effortless grace, their enormous bodies gliding over the waves. The sight is enough to make everyone feel joyful and excited.

Humpback Whale on the way to Antarctica

As you head back from the balcony, you can take in the nature display you just watched and reflect on how the whales dove for the final time before raising their tails in a wonderful show.

The Whale, tail-up, plunges headfirst into the ocean

The whales aren't the only amazing things you see when you snap pictures of this experience. A few magnificent birds like *Black Brown albatrosses,* along with *Southern Giant Petrel* and *Cape Petrel,* appear, adding an air of otherworldliness with their large wingspans and graceful flight. You fire away, capturing them in the middle of the vast ocean.

The ship has now docked near *Elephant Island*, an uninhabited island located about 250 kilometres northeast of the northern tip of the *Antarctic Peninsula*.

Geologically speaking, *Elephant Island* is a piece of the Scotia plate, which was formed from the continental fragments that originally connected *South America and Antarctica*. Along its coast, this rocky island—features a variety of rock types, including green and blue phyllites, blue schists, and green schists. They apparently gave it the moniker because of the frequent sightings of *Elephant Seals* by early explorers.

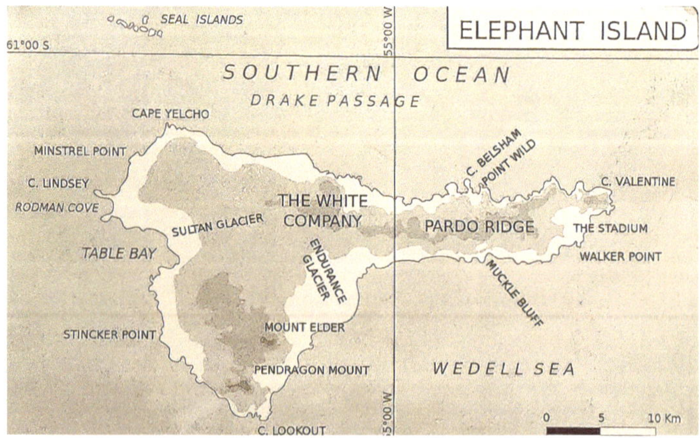

The Map of Elephant Island

For the previous two days and nights, you have been encircled by an endless sea. Seeing land again is a welcome sight, but also a sobering reminder of how life can persevere itself in the face of enormous adversity.

Anchored less than a kilometer away from *Elephant Island*, the guests have time to appreciate the untamed splendour of this wilderness, where imposing ice formations and precipitous cliffs attest to the might of Mother Nature.

Elephant Island

But, because of the continent's freezing temperatures and icy conditions, Antarctica has a monochromatic natural vegetation. Temperatures consistently below freezing and a lack of precipitation contribute to a hostile environment. Despite these challenges, many forms of life have evolved to thrive here. In the few ice-free areas, called *Oases*, a variety of mosses, lichens, and algae are seen to survive.

Amazing discoveries, filled with engaging interactions, breathtaking wildlife, and stunning landscapes, await you on this journey that is bound to leave you in awe of the unique wonders of this remote part of the world.

Scott, the expedition's seasoned leader, is hoping to use *Zodiac boats* to make an unanticipated landing on *Elephant Island*. The guests could set foot on this faraway continent thanks to these compact, inflatable motorboats, noted for their agility and ability to negotiate diverse water conditions.

Zodiac Boat

The expedition team has formally begun with the preparations. When the weather changes, everyone's emotions get torn between delight and alarm. The gusts of wind have suddenly picked up to dangerous levels, and any guests who venture out could be in danger.

The Zodiacs could swamp in the waves or encounter other difficulties on their journey, and this causes concern. It's disappointing for the tourists who planned to explore the island up close. It's difficult to argue with the fact that safety must be the primary priority in a situation as perilous as this.

To preserve the safety of the expedition members, *Scott* makes the difficult choice to abandon the landing. The expedition staff informs the dismayed passengers of the decision to cancel the landing with their reason.

Upset but reflective, the visitors retreat to their suites, their spirits albeit undimmed by this unfortunate setback. As soon as the captain is made aware of the expedition team's report, he sets sail for the *Antarctic Sound* as originally planned.

Guests congregate on the decks as the ship moves, soaking in the stunning scenery of Antarctica. Glacial features sparkle like gems in the sun, while seals and penguins can be seen going about their happy business on the ice seas.

Antarctica Landscape along the way

Although the unforeseen circumstances forced the landing on *Elephant Island* to be cancelled, the expedition so far has been filled with remarkable adventures and breathtaking views. Anticipation nonetheless mounts for the unknowns that await the adventurers of this remarkable voyage in the *Antarctic Sound.*

The ocean's surface now has a wonderful iridescent sheen thanks to the sun's warm rays. The grandeur of the setting is extremely mesmerizing. Seeing a July Antarctic sunset like this makes you feel like you've been transported to another time and place.

Captivating landscapes along the way,

You and the other passengers have once again returned to Deck 5 to know the itinerary for the next day. The team religiously fills you in on all the upcoming adventures and sights to could see on the *Antarctic Peninsula*. From encounters with rare and unusual species to views of beautiful landscapes, the possibilities seem unlimited.

The more of the briefing you absorb, the happier and more honored you feel to be a part of this journey. You may step into Antarctica's sacred soil tomorrow, the seventh continent that perhaps maintains an aura of mystery and enchantment.

With the Summer Antarctic Sunset staying in your thoughts, you travel back to your suite, anticipating the exciting adventures still to come on the Antarctic Peninsula.

Antarctica Awakens on Day 4

It is currently 5:30 AM. The excitement of the day ahead is enough to pull you out of bed without an alarm. Silver Cloud Ship's reassuring hum can be heard clearly whilst it ploughs through the icy water.

The first thing you see opening your cabin curtains as the sun begins to peek over the horizon is a spectacular white landscape speckled with icebergs.

View from the suite's veranda

The present moment is one worth savouring. *Antarctic Sound* is a huge, pristine area, with snow-capped mountains dotting the horizon in the early morning light. It's the scene that makes your heart race with an exhilarating mix of wonder and excitement because of its breathtaking scale and natural splendour.

As the ship sails on, small and tiny icebergs, called *Brash Ice*, dot the otherwise deep blue ocean-like jewels. They follow one another, enhancing the enigmatic appeal of the water and the developing landscape.

For a few breath-taking seconds, you do nothing except stare in awe as this floating palace glides majestically toward *Antarctic Sound*.

The ship has now entered *Antarctic Sound* and has anchored itself at a place known as *Brown Bluff*, the time is 7:30 a.m. *Brown Bluff* is a distinctive landform, a product of geological formation, an incredible basalt tuya, in the northern Antarctic *Tabarin Peninsula*.

This flat, extinct volcano, likely formed around a million years ago, is an incredible artefact of the past times. It all seemingly started with a volcanic eruption below the frozen surface of an englacial lake. Understanding its flaming past stands in stark contrast to the current coolness. A silent reminder of Earth's volatile, volcanic past that adds a layer of intrigue to your travel.

Meeting a colony of *Adelie penguins* is a lovely way to be introduced to the Antarctic's biodiversity; their black and white bodies shine out against the snow, making you feel like monochrome notes on a sheet of music. The normally silent scenery has come to life thanks to their unique social behaviour and inquisitive temperament.

Lively Adelie Penguins against a beautiful iceberg

You've just finished eating a substantial breakfast and putting on all your warmest clothes, your anticipation building until the announcement over the PA system says, "The weather is still unfavorable."

The erratic weather in Antarctica poses a constant threat to your enthusiasm for exploring this historical region. The fear that your landing might be called off is constant. Strong winds that aren't expected might also make this task dangerous. The level of dismay has risen, yet the imperative to put security first drives home once more the respect that this wild, untamed place commands.

The captain has aborted the expedition since, contrary to his hopes, the gust of wind has increased rather than subsided. Even in the backup location of *Hope Bay*, the winds are too severe to allow passengers to land.

Despite the setbacks, it is comforting to see a flock of *Adelie penguins* at a distance, gracefully soaring overhead. The white bands around their eyes only contribute to the cuteness of these 1840-discovered critters.

Adelie Penguins

The *Adelie penguin* is one of five different penguins that can be found in Antarctica. Other penguin species include *the Emperor, Gentoo, Chinstrap,* and *Macaroni Penguins*. Alas, *leopard seals* are their principal predators, robbing breeding colonies all along the Antarctic coast, especially on small islands and rocky outcrops, of their eggs and chicks.

As mentioned, *Chinstrap penguins* are one of several species of penguins you may encounter on your travels. A distinctive feature of these penguins is a narrow black stripe that runs across their foreheads. *Gentoo Penguins*, the largest of the penguin species may be identified by their vivid red or orange beaks and are just as striking.

You spot a colony of *Gentoo Penguins* waddling across a flat iceberg, their tails extending out behind them and sweeping from side to side, giving them the scientific name *Pygoscelis,* which means '*rump tailed*'.

You can see some of them plunging into the ocean for a refreshing swim. These rapidly decreasing penguin species are the quickest underwater swimmers of all penguins, capable of swimming up to 36km per hour.

Gentoo Penguins along the way

On the fourth day of your Antarctic journey, you have experienced a mixture of expectancy, discovery, and the desire to travel further into this uncharted, freezing wilderness, thanks to a tempting view of the Antarctic Sound.

The next day, you'll head to *Curtiss Bay*, where a whole new journey and a set of new discoveries lie in wait.

Day 5

Curtiss Bay, on the Antarctic Peninsula's northern shore, is a beautiful stop for travellers heading south. Having both of today's wonderful excursions with *Trinity Island* within easy reach has you bursting at the seams with excitement.

Silver Cloud at Curtiss Bay

These islands are a paradise for explorers thanks to their bizarre landscape of craggy peaks, snowy slopes, and unexplored ice fields. You can't take your eyes off the ice crystals that are growing in various shades of turquoise.

The beginning adventure involves a sloppy touchdown in *Curtiss Bay*.

The legendary expedition crew will perform a crucial ritual for you before your maiden voyage.

They want you to wear the allotted parka on top of your regular clothes. Next, you'll carefully pick up your leased gumboots from the cuff of your suit and make your way down to Level 3's *mud room*, where you'll change into them.

This inner sanctuary is a transformative zone. You can let your everyday shoes dream of the next steps as they repose in one of the open cupboards. The sturdy gumboots then find their correct place on your feet as you make your way toward the waiting Zodiac, eager to embrace the wild adventures that lie ahead.

But lo! When one of your daring missions is over and you've returned home safely, you must submit to a thorough decontamination. In order to rid yourself of the dust and the penguin's playful mischief, you must first visit the same mud room, the holy spot of metamorphosis and cleansing. Use the facility's powerful jet spray machines and robust brushes to remove the dust and evidence of the penguin's antics from your boots, bags, trekking poles, and other gear.

You'll be very meticulous about this process, making sure that no speck of grime or dust remains to tarnish the glory of your heroic journey. And once the cleansing symphony concludes, you shall don your cherished footwear once again, reestablishing your bond with the deck of the ship.

Thus, the expedition's ritual weaves together a tapestry of magic, combining function with reverence, and ensuring that each step taken and returned conveys the majesty and resilience of those who dare to explore the unknown.

So, after the mandatory mudroom ritual, you board a Zodiac and cruise to the coast, soaking in the untouched grandeur of the polar landscape along the way.

Boarding the zodiac boat

Zodiac boats on the way to Curtiss Bay

Feelings of exhilaration and ecstasy wash over you as you set foot on the Antarctic land for the first time. Snow-capped mountains rise majestically in the distance, and the tranquil bay stretches out before you. The air is crisp and pleasant thanks to the nearby sea.

Near Curtiss Bay

Enjoying sufficient time to soak in the spectacular scenery, it's time now to embark on the zodiac tour of the glacier.

You and your fellow tourists have boarded a fleet of Zodiac boats and are travelling around an adjacent island, where you marvel at the enormous and beautiful tabular icebergs as the zodiac skitters carefully around them.

The female captain of the boat expertly maneuvers the boat so that you may get the best possible views of the otherworldly scenery.

Glacial behemoths are a sobering reminder of nature's raw power and a source of wonder. In a short amount of time, massive icy mountains materialize, encased in a thick layer of ice and standing firm as sentinels of the Arctic realm.

Large iceberg near Curtiss Bay

Aside from the occasional crackling of ice and the far-off calls of seagulls, the farther the zodiac goes into this icy wonderland, the quieter it becomes. You will be captivated by the symphony of cold and solitude in a way that no other music can.

After returning and passing through the mudroom, with gumboots in your hands, as you leave—a tangible reminder of the life-altering potential of exploration crosses your mind—the gumboots shall now stay waiting to be reunited at the same corner of your suit until the next adventure arrives.

After a satisfying meal, the afternoon will be spent zipping about *Spert Island*.

Seated comfortably within the zodiac, you look out over a scene as picturesque as ever. A stunning new world awaits you at as you navigate through the island's breathtaking ice, rock, and waterscape. Adorable *Chinstrap penguins* can be seen doing their funny waddling thing and making everyone around smile. Against the backdrop of Antarctica's icy cliffs and mountains, these birds represent resilience and fortitude in the face of adversity.

Chinstrap Penguins

Over the course of the hour-long journey, the magnificence of *Spert Island* gradually reveals itself, like the pages of a storybook that unveil a new chapter with each turn. In the soft sunlight, these white cliffs take on a unique hue that will leave you gaping.

As the sun sets on another day in Antarctica, you can't help but reflect on all the amazing experiences you've had here. Antarctica's beauty and majesty, whether experienced on the exhilarating Zodiac rides, in the spectacular scenery, or during the wet landing at *Curtiss Bay*, have left an unforgettable impact on your soul and serve as a reminder of the infinite riches that exist on our planet.

Antarctic Shag, also referred to as imperial/king cormorant, is the only species of the cormorant family found in Antarctica.

Crossing the Lemaire Channel on Day 6

On the sixth day of the voyage, you get up bright and early, feeling a subtle flutter of excitement in your chest as you grab your camera and head to the ship's open-air deck. From here, you will have a front-row seat to the fabled crossing of the *Lemaire Channel*, a sight said to be unrivalled in its beauty and sheer audacity.

Prepare yourselves for a visual feast as the ship, a behemoth of steel and force, skillfully navigates its way through the vast mass of icebergs.

Crossing the Lemaire Channel

The sight of the perfect play of light and shadow on the pristine white icebergs dotting the crystal-clear waters curled down between towering cliffs sends shivers down your spine; crossing this channel, presumably, is a tribute to the triumph of humans over the challenges of nature.

Having accomplished its daring task, the ship finally comes to rest on the tranquil *Pleneau Island*, a tribute to the island's absolute splendour and serenity. You can prepare your senses for a really spectacular encounter.

Pleneau Island, less than a mile long, is located at the southern end of the *Lemaire Channel*, just off *Hovgaard Island*, west of *Booth Island*.

Silver Cloud at Pleneau Island

After enjoying a hearty breakfast, you are about to embark on another zodiac tour, this time across a tranquil landscape strewn with icebergs.

From your vantage point on the zodiac, the stunning icebergs lazily floating on the sea's glassy surface and emitting an unusual spectrum of blue captivate you.

Icebergs at Pleneau Island

As the Zodiac boat slices through the icy waters of the Southern Ocean, you can feel the chill in the air seeping into your bones, a stark reminder of the unforgiving environment that surrounds you. The sheer, towering cliffs of *Pleneau Island* loom ahead, their stark, jagged beauty both mesmerizing and foreboding. The boat's engine rumbles softly, carrying you closer to this remote outpost in the heart of Antarctica. With every passing moment, the icy wilderness unfolds before your eyes, a pristine world untouched by human hands. The anticipation in the air is palpable as you approach the ice-laden shore, where penguins waddle and seals bask, welcoming you to a land where nature reigns supreme, and every adventure is a brush with the extraordinary.

Soon, you are amidst a colony of penguins, and the thrill of watching such magnificent creatures up close is inexplicable. While some penguins are waddling around near you, others can be seen plunging headfirst into the crystal-clear waters below, presumably in quest of a fishy breakfast.

Gentoo penguins at Pleneau Island

After a quick but exciting adventure, it's impossible to avoid thinking about the amazing penguins you saw while on the way back to shore. Just as you are about to reach the shore, you're thrilled to see three enormous *Antarctica Fur Seals* lounging on the ice beyond.

The seals look curious and watchful, with their large, bulging eyes following every motion of the humans among them. You keep a respectful distance, not wanting to trespass on their space while continuing to admire their size and grace. The juxtaposition of their gigantic figures and the ice backdrop has created an enthralling image.

Antarctica Fur Seals

You stare in astonishment for a few moments before turning back to the waiting zodiac that will take you and the other guests back to the ship. This voyage has definitely been full of exceptional moments and surprising interactions, and you can't wait to share them with your fellow passengers back on the ship.

It is now 11.30 a.m., and the ship has awakened from its slumber to set sail once more, this time for *Petermann Island*, a hidden gem in the neighborhood. Anticipation is building once again as you prepare for another adventure in the heart of this frigid wilderness.

Given the close proximity to *Pleneau* and *Petermann Islands*, the captain has wisely decided to have the zodiacs follow the ship rather than lift them back on board.

Zodiac boats following Silver Cloud

Your palms are sweating as you cram your parka, gumboots, sweater, and camera into a water-resistant backpack and get ready to board the zodiac boat at 2:00 p.m. An amazing opportunity you've always wanted: to land yet again on the beautiful *Antarctic Peninsula*.

At 3.30 in the afternoon, the joy and excitement of being on the world's seventh continent flood back into your senses as you set foot on *Petermann Island*. The gentle rain isn't putting you off; in fact, it's adding to the sense of adventure and mystery, and making you feel even more at one with Antarctica's wild, untamed nature.

Climbing over rocky outcrops and establishing your footing cautiously, you slowly make your way over the landscape, enjoying the pleasant crunch of your boots on the newly revealed snow as you go.

Petermann Island is relatively small *(about 1 square kilometer)* and is characterized by rugged, rocky terrain, partially covered by snow and ice offering panoramic views of the surrounding glaciers and mountains that more than make up for its small size.

On the Island

Further exploration reveals a *refuge house*, a solitary monument against the wide white landscape said to have been erected in 1955 by the Argentinean government and ornamented with a cross as a silent homage to the three young lives lost here in 1982. This hut has a sombre past, reminding us of the sacrifices made by those who ventured here in the face of such a harsh and unforgiving environment.

Refuge Hut

When you stop to reflect, you can't help but notice the colonies of *Gentoo* and *Chinstrap penguins*, whose black and white plumage stands out beautifully against the freezing terrain, adding a welcome dash of life and colour. Each step they take, every slide on the treacherous ice, is a testament to their unyielding determination and the indomitable spirit that courses through their veins.

Watching these magnificent birds waddle and glide with graceful determination, you can't help but feel a deep connection to the unforgiving beauty of this pristine land. The icy waters into which they plunge are a metaphor for life's challenges, where only the strong and the resilient dare to venture. You are privileged to witness this epic battle, a thrilling saga of survival that plays out before your very eyes.

In this moment, you realize you are not just a spectator, but a witness to a grand spectacle of nature. The heart-pounding drama of life and death, survival and sacrifice unfolds before you, leaving you in silent awe of the untamed wilderness and the remarkable creatures that call it home.

Gentoo Penguins, stand as true masters of the frigid seas. With their streamlined bodies and powerful flippers, they are accomplished divers, able to navigate the cold, turbulent waters of Antarctica with remarkable finesse.

In their relentless quest for sustenance, *Gentoo Penguins* showcase their incredible adeptness at foraging. They possess an innate understanding of the ocean's depths, profound knowledge that has been honed over countless generations. When they embark on their underwater expeditions, it's as if they enter a world of enchantment beneath the ice. Their pursuit is a ballet of survival, a dance of hunger and agility beneath the unforgiving surface.

Gentoo penguins at Petermann Island

For a while, you focus intently, observing their every move. Their raucous cries combine with the crashing of the seas to create a beautiful symphony that captures the untouched nature of Antarctica.

Among the intriguing penguins on *Petermann Island* are *Weddell seals* (Leptonychotes weddellii) seen relaxing on the ice close. These huge and muscular seals with sleek, blubber-covered bodies are easily identified by their dark grey to brownish-black coats and distinguishing features.

Despite their mild and tranquil nature, these seals display an endearing and docile appearance. However, their big, curious eyes belie their calm demeanour.

Weddell Seal at Petermann Island

When you eventually say goodbye to *Petermann Island*, you will take along found memories of the refuge cabin, the penguins, seals and the insatiable drive for exploration that Antarctica instils in its visitors.

As you get closer to the coast, you can see the Zodiac boat patiently waiting for you, bobbing gently in the chilly waters. You get on board, feeling a mixture of amazement and exhilaration at interacting with the penguins. While the crew steers the Zodiac boat away from *Petermann Island*, deftly navigating the steep rocks and frigid waters, you go over some images and videos to re-create the amazing antics of the *Weddell Seals* and *Gentoo Penguins*.

On reaching, the crew helps you out of the zodiac and onto the sturdy deck, from where you head back to your cabin crossing the mudroom

Both *Pleneau Island* and *Petermann Island*, visited today, are beautifully scenic sections of the Antarctic Peninsula region, a remote and stunning part of *Antarctica*. These islands' unique features and the incredible natural beauty that characterizes the entire *Antarctic Peninsula* offer an authentic and awe-inspiring Antarctic experience. It provides incredible opportunities to witness the continent's pristine natural beauty and the resilience of its wildlife in one of the most remote and extreme environments on this Earth.

Day 7: Detaille Island

On the seventh day, you're just as psyched as you were on the first day of this Antarctic excursion. Today you will spend the day on *Detaille Island*, a tiny landmass off the northern tip of the Antarctic Peninsula and a part of *Palmer Archipelago*. You can't wait to get out and see the sights in this picturesque and historically significant region.

Stepping out onto the balcony of your suite, you'll be greeted with a stunning panorama of the pristine white landscape beyond. The air is crisp and refreshing, with a mild chill befitting the polar region's remote location and wild beauty.

View from the ship

To keep you occupied while you wait, the expedition team has prepared a briefing to fill you in on the history of *Detaille Island* and the significance of *Base W*, a historic research site for the *British Antarctic Survey* on this island, as well as the likelihood of any wildlife observations.

From the ship's deck, passengers can observe *Detaille Island's* rocky shoreline and snow-covered rocks while listening to the expedition team's internal announcements detailing the island's geology and the native species who call it home.

Detaille Island

As the ship cruises through the frigid seas, passengers can witness *Adélie penguins* swimming and diving close to the ship, their lithe bodies gliding effortlessly through the water. It's a fantastic view that fills you with joy.

As the ship draws near *Detaille Island*, the expedition staff quickly gathers the groups to provide instructions for the wet-landing procedure before allowing the first group to board the zodiac.

At 8 a.m., the first group hops on the zodiac and heads out toward the island, expressions of amazement and excitement written all over their faces. Now it's your turn. As the expedition team calls for your group, you pack your camera and waterproof gear and head to the predetermined meeting site.

As usual, boarding the zodiac boat fills you with a sense of eagerness and anticipation of what lies ahead as it pulls away from the ship and begins the quick but thrilling voyage to *Detaille Island*.

The landing place here is exceptionally perilous and tough, so only those with a solid grip have a good chance to reach up.

As you reach the shore, you find that the snow is quite soft, making your feet sink several inches with each step.

To your right, you find this prefabricated hut that was built as part of the original *Base W*. Opened in February 1956; *Base W* operated for only one year until February 1957. Started as part of the *International Geophysical Year (IGY)*, it was an international initiative to better understand Earth's physical characteristics. A worthy effort conceived in the spirit of global scientific cooperation.

Base W

During this brief period, researchers and scientists from several countries collaborated on a wide range of scientific projects, sharing data and expertise to advance our understanding of the Antarctic.

As you move ahead, the stunning panorama of the landscape ahead truly lures you here. You can see *Weddell seals and Crabeater seals* in large numbers and even *leopard seals* around the area, with some lounging in the sun on the snow and others playfully frolicking in the icy waters. Rare and engaging snapshot opportunities like these make you feel truly happy.

View from the Detaille island

Weddell Seals

Crabeater Seal

Leopard Seal

One of them, a young seal, full of life and mystery, commands your attention as it swims acrobatically just a few feet away from you. You take a series of beautiful shots that capture its vitality thanks to your quick eye and shutter.

Perhaps sensing your interest, it surfaces from the depths to give you an intense gaze, which you capture just in time as it makes a final, graceful dive back into the ocean and disappears.

Eye contact with a young seal

The remarkable *Kelp Gull*, which has adapted to and even colonized the tough environment of *Detaille Island*, can be seen here amongst it all. *Kelp Gulls* in Antarctica play an interesting role in the complex ecosystem of this region, both as scavengers and as part of the avian community that interacts with penguin colonies and other seabirds.

Kelp Gulls

That these birds have persisted despite the harshness of their environment is evidence of their strength and adaptability. Their attractiveness lies in the stark contrast between their predominantly white plumage and the stunning black markings on their wings and orangish beaks.

You can see, presumably, a sleek and silver *crabeater seal* reclining gracefully on the edge of a floating iceberg in the vicinity. Its streamlined body, speckled with dark spots, stands out brilliantly against the pristine white ice.

With its head resting nonchalantly on the ice, it basks in the frigid Antarctic sun. The endless expanse of this frozen beauty truly embodies the serene solitude of this remote polar landscape.

Suddenly, out of the dimly lit water emerges a shadowy figure. It's the leopard seal, effortlessly gliding with graceful strokes of its powerful flippers. Its long, streamlined body seems like a masterpiece of aquatic design, enabling it to move swiftly and deftly through the icy waters of the ocean. Its dark, speckled coat glistens under the faint light, providing a stark contrast to the surrounding hue.

Leopard Seal underwater

Your heart races, not out of fear, but out of awe and admiration for this amazing creature and the extraordinary ecosystem it lives in beneath the ocean's icy surface.

Meanwhile, a young seal is seen struggling to get up onto the snowy island in the background. After several failed attempts, it succeeds, but not before giving you some splendid pictures for your collection and also serving as an inspiring lesson of perseverance.

Baby Seal attempting to climb over the Iceberg

As your moment on this frozen frontier approaches, your attention is irresistibly pulled towards the *Silver Cloud Ship*, seemingly ensnared in a surreal and awe-inspiring spectacle. The vessel appears to be suspended within a mesmerizing, dreamlike composition, cradled snugly between two colossal icebergs that defy belief. This enigmatic vision, so surreal that it could be mistaken for an optical illusion, becomes a vivid testament to the profound and haunting allure of this untouched wilderness. It beckons, promising an encounter with a world where reality blurs with the extraordinary, and nature's grandeur knows no bounds.

Silver Cloud Ship

After more than an hour on this icy frontier, you return to where the zodiac dropped you off, ascend to Deck 3 of the ship, and finally reach your cabin on Deck 7.

Your journey across *Detaille Island* has been a true visual feast, filled with a collection of precious experiences captured in time through your camera.

Based on the itinerary, the *"Polar Plunge"* event, a once-in-a-lifetime opportunity to jump into the frigid embrace of the *Antarctic Ocean*, is slated to take place at 11:30 a.m., and all brave souls on board this beautiful *Silver Cloud Ship* are gladly encouraged to participate.

Because safety is of the utmost importance, the highly trained expedition team aboard the ship has prepared to keep a close check on everything to ensure a safe dive.

After agreeing to this breathless adventure and filling out the paperwork, the valiant participants gather on Deck 3 in minimal attire to prepare for their cold encounter. There's a palpable buzz of excitement in the air as a long line of eager guests waits patiently to get in on the action.

Once the expert expedition crew has fastened a rope around each participant's waist, they will be instructed to climb out onto the platform and leap into the icy abyss surrounded by stunning icebergs while gripping the other end of the rope in their hand.

After you leap, the team immediately goes into action and has you safely back on the platform in under a minute. You get out of the refreshingly cool water and immediately run back to your room to shed your swimwear.

Guests on Silver Cloud undertaking Polar Plunge

You haven't simply gone for one brief dive in the ocean; you've embarked on an incredible journey, and when it's all over, you'll be awarded a certificate to show off to your friends as proof that you braved the *Antarctic* waters.

On this seventh day of your Antarctic cruise, you get to see some spectacular icebergs while recharging with a vegetarian lunch at *La Terraza*, one of the ship's finest restaurants, before preparing to take part in an educational lesson to learn about the various types of penguins and how to tell them apart.

Iceberg along the way

After hearing the expedition team's plans for the next day, you sit down to a lovely dinner and settle in for the night.

Your itinerary for the next two days includes visits to *Damoy Point* and *Port Lockroy* on *Goudier Island,* a small, low-lying isle, before heading to visit *Neko Harbour*, the day after, which is 33 nautical miles from *Port Lockroy.*

Day 8 on Goudier Island

Fine white flakes can be seen melting on the frost-kissed glass of your veranda window on day eight of your extraordinary voyage to the Antarctic's furthest reaches. Despite the subzero temperatures, daylight paints the outer world in a vibrant, chilly tableau. Today also promises your fourth landing on the Antarctic Peninsula, at a place called *Damoy Point*.

View from the ship

Feelings of elation and joy surge over you as the ship's intercom confirms at precisely 7:30 a.m. that your adventure excursion for the day will proceed as planned.

At eight o'clock in the morning, the presenters pick up where they left off, instructing passengers to put on their parkas, gumboots, and life jackets and make their way through the obligatory mudroom rituals to the ship's third deck, the official starting point of the day's excursion.

Damoy Point

In around half an hour, you'll reach the shores of *Damoy Point*, a small frozen island concealed by several meters of beautiful snow. It created a breathtaking spectacle, with large swaths of white snow and towering glaciers dominating the terrain.

Braving the icy waves and making your way to the top of this vast white expanse, with determination coursing through your veins, you notice a small collection of huts—remnants of the study groups that once sought shelter here.

Landing at Damoy Point

Anticipation escalates as you trek the remaining 500 meters to the Penguin Rookery in the chilly, crisp air. Over the soft, fluffy snow, a rookery full of *Gentoo Penguins* has assembled, looking absolutely gorgeous in their tuxedo-like plumage.

With an inherent sense of community, they form bustling colonies, displaying strong social bonds and cooperation in tasks like nest-building and chick-rearing. Their sounds, which sound like a series of trumpeting honks, reverberate throughout the landscape, providing both, a means of communication and a lovely symphony that perfectly captures the icy beauty of the Antarctic air.

Gentoo Penguins

A light snowfall is just spreading off in the distance, its fine flakes slowly drifting down from the cloudless, grey sky. As they twirl in the icy wind, snowflakes sparkle like tiny diamonds in the scattered sunlight that breaks through the overcast sky.

In stark contrast to the falling snow is the penguin rookery, a lively congregation of these endearing creatures. They continue on with their regular routines, seemingly unfazed by the light snowfall, waddling gracefully with an air of serene determination.

Gentoo Penguins

As you take in this peaceful penguin rookery surrounded by snow, wonder and awe overcome you. The gentle snowfall has transformed the already captivating view into a calm, otherworldly experience, forever imprinting the beauty of *Damoy Island's* landscape on your soul.

As the lens focuses, your fingers dance over the shutter, recording the stunning majesty of these Antarctic icons for all time. The combination of their goofy pranks, royal demeanour, and palpable spirit of togetherness permeates the air to form a symphony of visual poetry.

Demoy Point

Forty-five minutes later, you return to the shore braving the chilly wind. The *South Polar Skua*, a large, powerful bird with a reputation for opportunistic scavenging, is suspected of cracking a giant penguin egg you encounter along the road.

This penguin egg, once a beacon of optimism and the promise of a new life in the icy heart of the South Pole, now serves as a sad emblem of the unrelenting struggle for existence that unfolds here every day.

Penguin egg

South Polar Skua

After a day spent admiring the natural beauty, you and your fellow passengers are ready to relax and enjoy the ship's comfortable restaurant. An exquisite four-course meal, including fresh seafood, has been meticulously prepared for you and is waiting.

You have just finished a delicious meal and are now lounging in your suit, looking forward to your next exciting adventure—a wet landing at *Port Lockroy*.

You lie on your bed and enjoy the quiet, letting the anticipation build through the indications of imminent excitement.

At precisely 3 o'clock on this eighth eventful day of the Antarctic Odyssey, a call rings through the ship's passageways, summoning your group to Deck 3

After gathering your belongings, and walking through the customary mudroom, you and fellow guests file onto the Zodiac boats that will transport you all to the picturesque island of *Port Lockroy.*

Port Lockroy

Upon arrival, the expedition team's expert hands lead you swiftly up a succession of rocky outcrops, opening a gateway to the stunning grandeur of the snowy terrain beyond.

The fresh Antarctic air awakens your senses as you make your way down this ethereal road, regaling you with tales of the region's untouched grandeur. Eventually, you'll come upon *Port Lockroy* Antarctic Station, its doors flung open, revealing a treasure trove of mementoes, each one a reminder of this incredible world.

Port Lockroy Antarctic Station

A lovely flutter of *Gentoo Penguins* graces the terrain around this paradise of trinkets. While the females wait patiently for the birth of their young atop little pebbles and fragile stones, the males busily scurry about collecting tiny rocks to build a cosy home for their mates, a testament to their unflinching commitment.

In this place of tender devotion and the promise of new beginnings, time seems to stand still, and you give thanks for the opportunity to witness some of nature's most intimate rituals.

Female Penguin atop small pebbles

A male Penguin with a pebble

When your stay on this enchanted island ends, you reluctantly but gratefully make your way back to the ship.

The nighttime routine begins at 6:15, much like clockwork. You listen closely as the next day's activities are recounted, learning about the amazing locations awaiting you and the safety measures that are necessary to ensure a smooth landing.

A certificate bearing the combined signatures of the captain of the vessel and the expedition leader, serving as an official testament to your visit to and successful traversal of the awe-inspiring and deeply captivating Antarctic circle, is later sent respectfully to your suit.

Certificate

Your heart and mind are racing as you set sail for *Neko Harbor*, 33 nautical miles distant, where untamed beauty and incredible adventures are promised. A kaleidoscope of breathtaking scenery opens before your eyes as you travel, infusing your very being with the majesty of nature.

Tomorrow, expect to reach a new sacred section of this frozen paradise and welcome its untamed splendour with open arms.

Neko Harbour & Cuverville Island on Day 9

At 7:30 a.m. on day nine of its epic mission to Antarctica's White Continent, *Silver Cloud* stands anchored in *Neko Harbour*, an entrance on the eastern tip of *Graham Land*, specifically in *Andvord Bay*.

In the early 20th century, Belgian explorer *Adrien de Gerlache* made the initial discovery of *Neko Harbor*, which was named after a Scottish whaling schooner who worked in the area between 1911 and 1924 and aptly received the name *Neko* in tribute.

After you've finished your morning rituals at *LA Terraza*, you'll have a wet landing in *Neko Harbor*. The area surrounding the landing spot at *Neko Harbor* is filled with a mesmerizing array of icebergs ranging in size from tiny to large to enormous, creating a breathtaking scene around your ship.

Neko Harbour

Unfortunately, the increasing wind speed and the presence of massive icebergs in the water make an island landing seem risky at best today. If you take the chance and make it to the island, you may be stuck there for hours or even days if a massive iceberg crashes in your direction and blocks the way back.

Icebergs near Neko Harbour

Scott, as the leader of the expedition together with the ship's captain, decides against making this perhaps unsafe landing in order to ensure the safety of the guests.

Instead, the ship is headed toward *Cuverville Island* hoping to find better landing conditions there.

A small boat passing between these brilliantly dispersed icebergs creates a picturesque sight as the ship speeds through some breathtaking terrain on its way to the *Cuverville Islands*.

Small boat along the way

Soon after, you come across a separate cruise liner that looks similar to the one you're on but is owned by a different firm anchored near another island. Regrettably, the captain of your ship cannot travel there because regulations forbid two ships from being on the same island at the same time.

Another ship anchored near an Island

As the excursion unfolds, you find yourself amid an exhilarating spectacle: A majestic mother *Humpback whale*, accompanied by her spirited young calf, glides effortlessly through the boundless expanse of the ocean, directly before the ship. Consequently, the vessel grinds to a sudden, anticipatory standstill, as if holding its breath in reverence to this awe-inspiring display of nature's grandeur.

Humpback Whales

Humpback Whale

As expected, a surge of eager visitors swarm the front deck, seizing the opportunity to immortalize this captivating scene with their cameras. Amidst the crowd, photographers are on the hunt for that elusive moment, a coveted treasure for any serious photographer – the instant when the *Humpback whale* gracefully dives headfirst into the water, its tail rising in perfect alignment, known as the *'Tail Up shot'*.

Tails up shot

Tail up shot

The ship has arrived at *Cuverville Island*. Surrounded by the dramatic mountains and glaciers of the Antarctic peninsula, this 252-meter (826-foot) high rock island with a long single-pebbled beach at its base is at the entrance to the *Errera Channel* and is home to numerous penguins.

The expedition crew has sprung into action, diligently completing plans to ensure the secure conveyance of guests to this alluring location. Once the ship is safely anchored, they launched a small fleet of Zodiac boats to convey the passengers to the island's shore.

Cuverville Island

As the zodiac boats sail from the ship, the steady increase in wind speed and the start of light snowfall have added an element of adventure to your journey.

Unfazed by the weather, you marvel at the lovely snowflakes swirling all around you, adding to the ethereal atmosphere of your polar trek.

Full of anticipation and wonder, you cruise to *Cuverville Island*, eager to take part in any and all thrilling pursuits that await you there.

After disembarking the zodiac and walking through a piece of small rock beach and up onto the white expanse, you'll be greeted first by *South Polar Skuas*, followed by the frenzied activity of the several *Gentoo Penguins* who have made this area their home.

Gentoo Penguins on Cuverville Island

South Polar Skua

Gentoo Penguins of Antarctica's *Cuverville Islands* are known for a variety of endearing characteristics that distinguish them from other species. As previously observed, the vivid orange of their beaks and the flawless whiteness of their feathers make these birds stand out against the stark whiteness of their surroundings. The penguins here, however, are reputed for their vivacity and activity, which manifests itself in a broad range of exciting behaviours, from synchronized swimming to enthusiastic waddling through the rocky environment.

Gentoo Penguins **of** *Cuverville Islands*

Overall, the *Cuverville Islands'* playful *Gentoo Penguins* are a natural wonder, acting as a model of perseverance, community, and cheerful life in the face of adversity.

So, after spending about an hour in the frigid wind photographing these beautiful birds, you come back to the shore, jump back aboard the Zodiac, and return to the warm, familiar confines of the ship.

As the ship continues its journey through the icy waters, time slips away, and you find yourself in the midst of a mesmerizing dance with magnificent icebergs. Their breathtaking forms command your attention, forcing you to reach for your camera to capture these fleeting moments, preserving their awe-inspiring beauty for future generations to behold.

Icebergs along the way

You've just finished up a wonderful evening with some fascinating new friends at the Deck 4 Restaurant and have decided to call it a night.

The next morning, you'll get ready to set sail on an exciting trip that will take you to the last two stops on your voyage before bringing you back to *Port Williams* via the fabled *Drake Passage*.

Part 1 of Your Trip to Half Moon Island Begins Today, Day 10

As the first ethereal rays of dawn infiltrate the cabin, they reveal a mesmerizing spectacle that seizes your senses. The vessel, with a grace befitting a phantom, embarks on a tranquil voyage towards its first destination: the enigmatic *Half Moon Island.*

It glides as if guided by unseen forces, over the still, pristine waters, whispering tales of untold wonders waiting to be unveiled.

Reaching Half Moon Island

Half Moon Island is a crescent-shaped landmass located on *Livingston Island,* about 1.35 kilometers north of the *Burgas Peninsula* in the *South Shetland Islands archipelago,* and is the penultimate stop on your wonderful and intriguing Antarctic tour.

It is a small but significant section of the Antarctic Peninsula territory where *Chinstrap Penguins* dwell and breed. With its high, snow-capped mountains as a backdrop, this island paints a picture of spectacular splendour.

Half Moon Island

As the ship approaches another wonderful landing, you look out the window at the white landscape spread out in front of you, bathed in soft light. It foreshadows a great day.

The natural beauty of this island is immediately obvious the moment you set foot on it. A profound sense of awe and wonder envelops the very atmosphere as the captivating spectacle unfolding before you captivates your eyes. *Chinstrap Penguins*, with their distinctive black heads, waddle and frolic in their natural habitat.

These wondrous creatures of the icy realms, execute their delightful ballet with a flourish leaving an indelible mark on your heart. Their movements, as intricate as a carefully choreographed dance, fill your senses with an exquisite sense of wonder.

Chinstrap Penguins on Half Moon Island

Your gaze then shifts to the pristine wilderness of *Half Moon Island*, a canvas painted with nature's own brush strokes. Snowy peaks soar into the endless, crystalline sky, their towering forms casting imposing shadows upon the island's cerulean waters. It's a visual symphony of opposites, where the island's icy summits and the azure embrace of the sea stand in stark, magnificent contrast.

As you stand there, you find yourself transported to a realm seemingly untouched by time—a world where nature reigns supreme, unbridled, and untamed. It's a realm where the past meets the present, and the call of the wild still echoes in the wind.

But your journey through this ethereal landscape doesn't end there. Nearby, on the pristine expanse of ice, two colossal *Weddell Seals* bask in the rare warmth of the polar sun. Their massive, sleek bodies exude a commanding presence, a testament to their dominance in this icy kingdom. Against the backdrop of the immaculate terrain, their presence is an awe-inspiring reminder of the raw power and beauty that nature bestows upon this remote corner of the world.

You become a witness to the everlasting drama of nature's grandeur in every footstep, ripple, and elegant motion of its unique residents in this isolated refuge of life and contrast.

Weddell Seals at Half Moon Island

While you're busy shooting the island's fauna, some thrill-seeking tourists choose to kayak about Half Moon Island's frigid waters, apparently to get a fresh perspective of the island as well as to enjoy a one-of-a-kind experience and excitement

Guests of Silver Cloud Ship enjoy Kayaking

Venturing to the southern shores of *Half Moon Island*, they greet your senses with an extraordinary spectacle that epitomizes the eternal rhythms of the natural world. Here, nestled against the rugged terrain and the icy shoreline, lies the *Chinstrap Penguin* rookery—a living testament to the relentless cycles of life and nature's unyielding beauty.

Chinstrap Penguins with their chicks

A single Chinstrap Penguin with her chick

As you approach this bustling colony of *Chinstrap Penguins*, you can't help but feel an overwhelming sense of wonder. The air reverberates with a cacophony of lively chatter and the unmistakable scent of the ocean. Several of these charismatic birds have congregated here, each meticulously tending to their nests and their precious, fluffy chicks. It's a bustling metropolis of penguin families, a harmonious chaos of life that unfolds before your very eyes.

The sight is nothing short of awe-inspiring. Adult *Chinstrap Penguins*, adorned with their distinct black caps and elegant white plumage, dart back and forth, shuttling food to their hungry offspring. The chicks, covered in downy fluff, peep and chirp with insatiable curiosity, their oversized eyes peering at the world with boundless wonder.

The parent penguins, on the other hand, are extremely protective of their chicks and newborns and will fight any other penguin that comes too close.

Dare You- Mother Penguin to an Intruder Penguin

You can't help but wonder if it's displaying human-like maternal instincts, such as a ferocious protective display. The battle to survive in this hard but beautiful environment is palpable and becoming more apparent.

Suddenly, a male penguin attempts to jump atop the back of a female penguin, signifying the start of the mating ritual. Because male penguins lack a penis, a cloacal kiss transfers sperm, in which they pass the sperm from one cloaca *(a shared opening for excretion and reproduction)* to another. As a result, when you witness penguins in the wild, it can take several minutes for them to mate.

Mating of Chinstrap Penguins

You are so engrossed in preserving the core of this intriguing play of procreation and preservation of life in Antarctica that you become unconscious of passaging time.

The Chinstrap Penguin rookery on Half Moon Island is more than just a gathering of birds; it's a living embodiment of the cyclical dance of life, where generations come and go, and the relentless passage of time is marked by the comings and goings of these spirited birds. It's a vivid illustration of the profound connection between the natural world and the enduring forces that shape it. Standing here, you are privileged to witness this captivating chapter in the ongoing narrative of life in the heart of Antarctica.

When you discover you are the last person to leave this lovely beach, you gather your belongings and depart.

As you speed toward your zodiac, the breathtaking Antarctic landscape surrounds you, with the cold waters and snow-covered peaks providing a stunning backdrop.

In the midst of this stark beauty, you catch sight of a mother *Kelp Gull*, her striking black and white plumage standing out against the blue ocean as she stands protectively near her fluffy, down-covered *baby gull*. This little chick, equally stunning in its own way, is just another example of life's survival in this harsh environment.

Kelp Gull with her chick at Half Moon Island

And then, as if to complete the scene, a magnificent adult Kelp Gull soars stylishly overhead. Its outstretched wings, with the dark grey mantle contrasting against the pristine surroundings, capture the essence of freedom and grace that only a bird in flight can convey. The gull's yellow bill with a red spot shines like a beacon as it gracefully descends towards a rock nearby.

Kelp Gull at Half Moon Island

This moment epitomizes the raw, unadulterated beauty of Antarctica, where wildlife flourishes in a harsh world of ice and cold, creating a memory you'll treasure for the rest of your life.

Standing on Half Moon Island, your view of the Silver Cloud Cruise ship is nothing short of breathtaking. As you gaze out at the vast expanse of the Antarctic Sea, you see the majestic vessel anchored in the deep blue waters, contrasting beautifully with the pristine, icy surroundings.

Above, the sky is a mesmerizing display of cloud formations. Pillowy cumulus clouds hang low, their soft, marshmallow-like forms painted in shades of pink, lavender, and soft pastel blues by the setting sun, casting a warm, ethereal glow over the ship and the icy waters.

As you take in this scene from *Half Moon Island*, you're captivated not only by the grandeur of the *Silver Cloud Cruise* ship but also by the serene and untouched beauty of the Antarctic environment that surrounds it, making this moment unarguably an unforgettable experience.

Silver Cloud Ship viewed from Half Moon Island

You get off the zodiac and head back to your suit, eager to review and discuss your discoveries with the group, particularly those concerning the mating behaviours of the penguins.

As the day progresses, you realize that your time spent on *Half Moon Island* and with its endearing residents will be among your most cherished memories. However, the journey is not yet complete. As you enter the final stage of your journey into the pristine Antarctic environment, there is still a bit more to discover and possibly more beauty to enjoy.

After a delicious supper, you put away your photographic mementoes and go to work preparing for the day's second and last landing of your fantastic journey.

There's a tangible mix of excitement for what's to come and melancholy that this great trip will soon come to an end.

Day 10: Arrival at Yankee Harbor, Part 2

Amidst day 10 of this unforgettable expedition, you brace yourself for having finally reached the zenith of this odyssey. The atmosphere is crackling with electric anticipation. *Yankee Harbor*, a sanctuary cherished by eco-tourists and devoted wilderness enthusiasts alike, looms on the horizon.

In the air, you can practically taste the palpable excitement, like a symphony of heartbeats echoing through the vast expanse of this Southern Ocean. But, as you draw near, there is also a subtle undercurrent of bittersweet melancholy that lingers. It is a poignant reminder that the arrival at this remarkable haven marks the culmination of an unparalleled voyage to the ethereal *White Continent*.

This ship has just entered the inner port of *Yankee Harbor*, flanked by *Shopski Cove*, *Glacier Bluff*, and *Spit Point*. Standing on the southwest side of *Greenwich Island* in the *South Shetland Islands* off the coast of Antarctica, *Yankee Harbor* provides a relatively sheltered anchorage for ships, making it a popular destination for those travelling in the area. The surrounding landscape features glaciers, rugged coastlines, and a variety of wildlife, including penguins and seals.

You let your spirits soar and your hearts race as you savour these last moments of your extraordinary journey, for they shall remain etched with the indelible ink of adventure and the promise of memories that will forever course through your veins.

Yankee Harbour

Minutes later, you re-enter the Zodiac boat, dressed in your parka, life jacket, and gumboots, ready to face the island's freezing but thankfully dry weather.

When you land, you spot a few *Southern Elephant seals* lounging around; these creatures make excellent subjects for a close-up photograph, their distinctive features standing out against the harsh white Antarctic landscape.

Southern Elephant Seals

Every detail of this natural beauty is captivating, from the glaciers calving into the ocean to the icebergs drifting freely among the dazzling waves.

From a distance, you can make out a rookery of *Gentoo Penguins*. These *Gentoos* are just as protective of their young as the *Chinstraps* seen on *Half Moon Island*. A loud cry serves as a warning to any intruder, like a wandering penguin, to stay away from their young. Their devotion to their young dispels any doubt about their strong maternal instinct, making for a truly amazing sight.

Gentoo Penguins with their chicks at Yankee Harbour

As the sun casts its golden glow over the pristine landscape of *Yankee Harbour*, it becomes evident that the moment you have both yearned for and dreaded has arrived.

It is not a decision made lightly, the choice to bid farewell to this remote haven. There's heaviness in the air, a sense of reluctance that hangs like a cloud, as you grapple with the realization that this was your last landing in this frozen wilderness. Each step taken on the rocky terrain felt like a bittersweet farewell to an old friend, and the minutes ticked by like the sands of an hourglass, reminding you that time is running out.

You have gathered memories like treasures, savouring the sights and sounds of *Yankee Harbour* one last time. The playful antics of penguins, the haunting calls of seabirds, and the serene majesty of ice-capped peaks—all are imprinted in your minds with a poignancy that only the imminent departure can bring.

Reluctantly, you finally make your way back to the waiting Zodiacs. The icy Antarctic waters mirror the emotions within you—both frigid and deep. With each stroke of the oar, you shall inch closer to *Port Williams*, the final destination of your extraordinary Antarctic expedition.

But remember, as you leave behind *Yankee Harbour*, you also carry it with you in your hearts. The emotional bonds forged with this land of extremes, its rugged beauty, and the camaraderie of fellow travellers are all souvenirs that time cannot fade. Though you may depart, the spirit of Antarctica will forever reside within you, a reminder of the profound and transformative journey you embarked upon in this frozen wonderland.

The ship will spend the entire next day going through the *Drake Passage*, noted for its turbulent waves. The voyage will almost certainly be rough, with strong waves that may produce motion sickness. However, this is the culmination of an incredible journey and a genuine taste of Antarctica.

11th day: Passing through the Drake Passage

As the ship struggles to make its way through the perilous *Drake Passage* today, the over 5-meter-high waves, as expected, are wreaking havoc on the passengers. The howling wind and the crashing waves against the hull of the ship serve as an audible reminder of nature's unrestrained power, making seasickness an uncomfortable travelling companion for many.

Strong westerly winds known as the "Roaring Forties," "Furious Fifties," and "Screaming Sixties" seem to blow through this region which presumably is because of the Earth's rotation and the temperature differences between Antarctica and the equator.

Fortunately, there are stretches of stunning beauty sprinkled throughout the otherwise chaotic passage. Rainbows appear in the midst of the rough seas as sea foam sprays reflect the sun. Passengers' worries are replaced with wonder as they see the incredible play of light on the ocean's surface.

You, like the other passengers, have taken to eating in the privacy of your cabin to prevent the motion sickness brought on by the ship's incessant rocking.

The ship's captain, too, seems to share these feelings and displays an eagerness to pass through this rough patch by increasing the ship's speed.

Day 12

The *Drake Passage*, one of the world's most treacherous and infamous stretches of water, is now in your rearview mirror as of the morning of January 15, 2023. The memories of the enormous waves and the ship's constant swaying will however forever remain etched in your mind, but there is also a sense of accomplishment and pride in having made it through this passage and exploring Antarctica.

After what must have been a gruelling journey, passengers have emerged from their hiding places, their faces showing a mix of weariness and elation.

The *Drake Passage* is now more than just a geographical feature; it is a shared story that honours the perseverance of humans, a testament to the resilience of the human spirit and the insatiable desire to discover new things. Each traveller's story is unique because of how they reminisce about the range of emotions they experienced, from terror to excitement to shock. Maintaining the trip's transcendental significance in the traveller's imagination.

Following a hearty breakfast in one of the ship's restaurants, you'll begin packing your stuff to prepare for tomorrow's early morning disembarkation and flight return to Santiago.

After you've finished shopping on the ship's fifth deck, you head to the lounge for a more formal occasion. Guests on board would want to take this time to thank everyone on board, especially the ship's captain and expedition team members, without whom this experience would not have been nearly as remarkable.

Thanksgiving function on Silver Cloud

So, after one last meal with your travelling companions, you do as the ship's staff recommends; leave your bags outside your suite before retiring to your suite's bed for the ultimate time.

Day 13 is Disembarkation Day.

Sipping your morning tea in the *Silver Cloud's* dining room on the morning of the thirteenth and ultimate day of this fantastic adventure, you watch the ship slowly pull itself into *Puerto Williams Port*, its final destination.

Puerto Williams

As soon as you hear the announcement to depart from deck 5, you and your fellow passengers gather in a line to say their farewell, this time to the entire crew members of the ship. The team has attended to your every need throughout this fantastic voyage. Their dedication, expertise, and enthusiasm undoubtedly played a significant role in making your trip so memorable.

As soon as you step foot on dry land, a wave of nostalgia and gratitude washes over you; the adventure may be over, but the memories and lessons you learned during the last fortnight will last a lifetime.

As you look back on the ship, feelings of longing and yearning to return to the ship, the place you called home for a brief but spectacular time, are inevitable.

You hop on the waiting shuttle to *Port Williams Airport*, where a private jet will take you to *Santiago* in four hours.

As you head back to civilization, you think back on the range of feelings you experienced: from profound humility in the presence of nature's majesty to absolute delight because of the splendour all around. The icebergs you saw are incontrovertible evidence of the enormous forces that produced these frozen continents, with their tabular bergs, iceberg arches, and ever-changing ice formations.

The natural beauty of Antarctica will always remind you of your first glimpse of penguins waddling on the ice, seals snoozing in the sun, and whales breaching in the distance.

Amidst all this, it is imperative to keep in mind that Antarctica's vast ice sheet and its reflecting qualities play a crucial role in the global climate system. Because of their high albedo *(reflectivity)*, ice and snow help maintain the temperature of the planet by reflecting a large quantity of solar radiation back into space. The arctic air and sea that encircle Antarctica further cool the Southern Ocean and beyond.

The health and stability of the Antarctic ice sheet have serious effects on sea levels globally. Warming temperatures might cause substantial chunks of ice to melt, which would mark a sharp rise in sea levels, resulting in far-reaching and potentially disastrous effects for coastal regions all over the world.

Overall, the distinctive terrain, harsh climate, and enormous ice sheet of Antarctica have a significant influence on ocean currents, the earth's energy balance, global temperature trends, and climate dynamics.

As you wave goodbye to Antarctica from the air, your heart is full of precious recollections, fresh insights, and a profound respect for the delicate beauty of our world.

Antarctica has displayed its untamed beauty, strength, and fragility; it is a tribute to our world's enduring and awe-inspiring force. The Ice

Kingdom is the last remaining natural wilderness on this planet, and its beauty is brutal yet unforgettable.

Now that you've begun the long trek home, you know, with certainty, that you left a piece of yourself somewhere across the frozen wastelands of this seventh continent.

MY TRIBUTE TO THIS INCREDIBLE PART OF THIS PLANET:

In the Heart of the Earth, where icy winds whisper secrets of a world untouched by time, I found my soul forever changed. Antarctica, the seventh continent, a land of pristine beauty and untamed wilderness, has carved its indelible mark upon my very being. My words may fall short, unable to capture the magnitude of this frozen wonderland, but I must try, for Antarctica deserves every tribute, every ode, every heartfelt emotion that flows through my being.

I stand here, having just returned from a voyage that took me to the edge of the world. As I gazed upon the vast, ice-covered landscape, I felt an overwhelming sense of humility and awe. Antarctica, the last true wilderness on our planet, possesses a power that transcends human understanding. It is a place where time stands still, where the relentless march of progress has not yet left its mark.

The very air I breathed seemed to hold the secrets of the ages, whispering tales of survival against all odds. Antarctica is a realm of extremes, where the sun never sets in the summer and the winter nights stretch on forever. It is a place where life clings to existence in the harshest of conditions, where penguins waddle on ice floes, seals bask in the fleeting warmth, and whales breach the icy waters, defying the freezing depths below.

But it is not just the wildlife that makes Antarctica a place of wonder. It is the sheer, unadulterated beauty of the landscape itself. Towering icebergs, sculpted by nature's hand, glisten like diamonds in the unrelenting sun. Glaciers, ancient and eternal, flow like rivers of ice, carving valleys and fjords with patience that spans millennia. The air is crisp and pure, carrying the promise of a world untouched by pollution and human interference.

In Antarctica, I discovered a sense of peace that eludes us in the chaos of modern life. The silence is deafening, broken only by the crackling of ice and the distant calls of wildlife. It is a place where one can truly reconnect with the essence of our planet, where the fragility of life and the importance of preservation become self-evident truths.

As I stood on the frozen continent, I couldn't help but be moved to tears. Tears of joy for having witnessed such a magnificent place, tears of sorrow for the imminent threat of climate change, and tears of gratitude for the privilege of experiencing a land so pure and untouched.

My tribute to Antarctica is not just a reflection of my journey; it is a plea to the world. We must protect this sacred land, for it is a testament to the power and beauty of nature. Antarctica, with its endless horizons of ice and its timeless grandeur, is a reminder that we are but stewards of this planet. We must act now to ensure that this continent remains unspoiled for generations to come.

In the end, Antarctica is more than a place; it is a state of mind. It is a place that touches the soul, leaving an indelible mark that will forever remind us of the majesty of our planet. Antarctica, you are the seventh continent, but in my heart, you are the first and the last, a testament to the enduring wonder of our world.